HEART
and
HOME

Father Michael Cleary

CAMPUS PUBLISHING

ISBN 1 873223 60 9

First published May 1992

ACKNOWLEDGEMENT
The Author and Publishers are grateful to Independent
Newspapers Ltd. and Tribune Newspapers Ltd. for
permission to reprint these pieces.

Typeset by Irish Typesetters, Galway
Printed and bound in the Republic of Ireland

Published by
Campus Publishing Limited
26 Tirellan Heights
Galway
Ireland

Contents

Foreword

I have to thank Kevin Brophy again. He took a pile of dog-eared magazines and newspapers containing articles written by me over the years and, from them, put together a book called **From The Heart**. Now he has managed to find enough material for a second book.

Apparently there are a lot of people who like to read simple articles about their faith and its application to day-to-day life.

We have called this new book **Heart and Home** because I believe that *heart* and *home* are the two most basic elements in building a Christian society.

As with my first book, I do not write for scholars or theologians, but I pray that **Heart and Home** will give hope, encouragement and comfort to ordinary people who are trying sincerely to follow Christ's teachings in their daily lives.

Father Michael Cleary
Dublin
May 1992

Cover Portrait

In 1992 Father Michael Cleary was the recipient of the annual award of the Performing Artists Trust.

Previous winners included Noel Purcell, Val Doonican and Maureen Potter.

Our front-cover portrait was commissioned by the PATS from Dublin artist, Pat Phelan and is reproduced with their kind permission.

Rumours of My Death . . .

It was a strange week, that week when a rumour spread like wildfire that I was dead! Reporters phoned to check on the news and one paper had even got some photos of me out of their files in readiness for my obituary. A minute's silence was observed for me in a Dublin dance hall.

The first I really knew about it was when I appeared on the altar for Mass that Monday and some of the congregation applauded and cheered. I looked so obviously puzzled that one woman shouted up to me: "We thought you were dead."

I got numerous phone calls from friends I hadn't heard from in a long while and when I asked if they had heard the rumour they sheepishly admitted that it was the reason for their call.

Of course, I've had a few laughs from it and particularly from the variety of ways in which I was supposed to have expired. I was touched too by the sincere relief and joy of so many to find that the rumour was untrue, but the fact that it could be true did set me thinking.

None of us has a lease on life and death can come at any time. While we all accept the inevitability of death and we see the lives of others cut off suddenly, so frequently, and in so many different ways, it's amazing how little consideration we give to the fact that it could happen to ourselves. Very few of us can honestly say like Pope John: "My bags are packed."

Apart from the fact that I love life, I'm certainly glad that the rumour was untrue. Spiritually I'm sure I would like to have been much better prepared and I know I would have left a lot of trouble behind for others who would have to sort out the mess of my affairs.

I would have left behind an out-of-date will, unpaid bills, unanswered letters, unfulfilled promises and apologies not made, a desk and drawers filled with jumbled-up papers, accounts, indecipherable notes and memos and a filing system unknown to anyone but myself.

I also thought about the things I would have liked to be remembered by and the recommendations my friends could have made to God for me in their prayers. I amazed myself with the number of achievements and honours that I strove so hard for and which I now had to discard as of no value in this type of accounting. Medals won, positions held or bank balance, would not impress St. Peter.

I only hoped that some people could honestly say to God that I had eased their burdens a little or brought them a little closer to Him—that the world had been a little better for the fact that I had passed through it. I can tell you, it was a valuable exercise.

It is so easy to confuse the important with the unimportant and to concentrate on the dramatic and glamorous while neglecting the monotonous routines that are of real value.

The rumour made me look back and look forward. It is good to look back and learn from mistakes—to look at the map and check our location and our destination and whether we have deviated from the road and to make the necessary corrections to get back on its solid surface, to remind ourselves that the attractive scenery along the way is there to be admired and to give pleasure but never to lure us off course or to distract our attention so much as to cause a crash.

The life that God gave me has only one real purpose. It also has a real importance because of that purpose. If I am to use it properly I must be constantly aware of both. Phrases from the scriptures should always be in our minds: "You know not the day nor the hour" and St. Paul's: "If I have the voice of angels . . . but have not love I am nothing."

You shouldn't be frightened by this sort of meditation. Death should not be feared. It should be lived for. The gentle babe in the crib will remind us of this because He came precisely to take the fear out of death.

6

The Day I Had to Choose Between God and Football

Young people need desperately to develop the ability and habit of thinking and making judgments for themselves, and they also need very much the confidence and courage to act on their own judgment, particularly when they find themselves alone in situations when no reliable advice or guidance is available.

It is amazing how seldom even adults think for themselves. We so easily follow fashions or trends without questioning them. When someone in the fashion world clicked his fingers, all the ladies jumped obediently into miniskirts, without taking a look in the mirror at the pair of legs they were displaying.

With equal obedience they then switched to maxis, staggered around in stiletto heels, and ended up wearing orthopaedic boots and shoes. Supermarkets employ psychologists and run marketing seminars to study the psychology of the shopper so that he or she will slavishly buy the product being pushed rather than that which might be their own choice.

How much easier is it to influence young people in directing their thinking about pop stars, fashion, records, etc? I am not too worried when it is simply a case of extracting money or loyalty from young people by commercial interests, but I am very worried when it comes to decisions that affect their careers, their future and their immortal souls.

It is important that young people should question values, and be able to discern, evaluate, and reject the pressures and sham that surround them.

For example, I would say to a young person: "Don't buy a record simply because it is the top of the charts. Listen to it, and judge it for yourself, and then buy or reject it."

It is important that young people should realise that the fact that a record hits the top does not necessarily mean that it is the considered choice of the majority. Very often it is the one that certain powerful people decide is going to reach the top, and they have the machinery and the power to make it happen. I am not making a particular attack on the record industry. It is just a convenient example of the high pressure and tactics that are used in so many fields to manipulate young people without any regard for their material, moral or spiritual welfare.

I like young people to question religion, and its practice, and the teachings of their church, as well as everything else.

Even when young people do think and make judgments, it is not easy to act on those judgments. They need a lot of confidence and courage. It is so much easier to go with the mob. Uncertainty, insecurity, inability to explain, and the desire to be accepted are all a part of the teenage years, and militate greatly against independent action.

I find it hard to believe now that I was reluctant to tell my schoolpals that I was thinking of the priesthood. I was genuinely afraid of being jeered or having to explain my decision.

As a small boy I passed Dominick Street church on my way to and from school. Usually I was accompanied by a pal, and years later as adults, recalling our schooldays, we discovered that whenever we were alone we each went in to say a prayer, but together we were two tough men smoking butts and didn't even bless ourselves passing, because it would seem so "square".

If one of us had the intelligence and courage to do the "square" thing, we would have helped each other.

This happens so often with young people and if only some had the courage to do what they believe is right, they would not only direct their own lives in the right direction, but would help others to do so as well. Rather than follow the mob in possibly the wrong direction, they would become leaders of others simply by doing their own thing when they know it is the right thing.

This applies to attitudes, too, and use of drink, drugs, sex, money, leisure, studies, savings, marriage, and so many other factors that can enhance or wreck young lives.

A young person preparing for life is like an athlete pursuing an Olympic medal. The athlete has many other intermediate goals in life, but their importance and his pursuit of them are very much influenced by the ultimate goal and they will never be allowed to interfere with or hinder his achievement of that medal.

It is important then that the ultimate goal of life be decided before leaving school. I suggest that the only imperishable reward and ultimate goal is salvation. Life is a success or failure, depending on how we face our final exam. "What does it profit a man to gain the whole world and suffer the loss of his soul."

God has given us many good things in life for our use and enjoyment and we should use and enjoy them, but never to the extent that they divert or distract us from our ultimate purpose. Motivation is the key.

Only if we know God and love Him enough will we be able to make the sacrifices that a romance with Him demands. When we are young, some things can become so important to us, that we do let them take over our attention, to a degree that can be dangerous and, at times, fatal.

I remember a very important football game I was chosen to play in. I was in the Seminary, and football was really more important than God to me at the time. Indeed, I gave it more attention than I gave my prayers or studies. I was refused permission to play in this important match and, even though I knew it would mean expulsion, I thought very seriously of defying the authorities. Thank God, I had some good friends who talked sense into me.

It was the blackest day of my life, as I could hear the roar of the crowd in Croke Park, and had not even a radio to tell me what I was missing. Now I look back, and it all seems so unimportant. I might have a medal rusting in a drawer now, but I would have sacrificed my vocation and career and maybe even that match? And who cares about it now?

I have had over 30 years of a happy fulfilled priesthood and I hope I am still on course for salvation. My sacrifice which seemed too much to ask for at the time seems very small now, when compared with the many blessings and rewards the priesthood has brought me.

Looking back, it was a test of my love. My love for God and my love of football were in competition and one had to win. Love can only be enjoyed and given fully when there is no competition. God may be a jealous lover, but I have found that He is the greatest Lover. It frightens me to think that in my immaturity I almost missed out on this and blamed Him for being too demanding.

"Hump the Red Hair— We'll Keep the Baby."

One of the nicest experiences I have had in my work as a priest started off as a potentially very nasty and difficult one.

A lady came to me in a state of near hysteria. She was a married woman. Her panic was due to the fact that the child she was expecting had been fathered not by her husband, but by a neighbour.

It took a while to calm her down and it was obvious that she was a good woman who, out of loneliness, succumbed very briefly and foolishly to the attentions of another man. It was completely out of character for her to do so.

You might say it was a once-in-a-lifetime brainstorm but she was now paying a terrible price for her brief flirtation. She was an honest woman and would not try to bluff her husband. She had thought of running away and even thought of suicide but, funny enough, had not thought of abortion.

We talked for a long time and eventually arranged that she would give her husband his favourite meal that evening and have a nice fire lighting and that I would arrive when he was at his mellowest and that she would withdraw quietly to the kitchen while I broke the news.

I didn't look forward to the task but I arrived armed with a few prayers and all kinds of brilliant arguments.

Paddy (we'll call him that) was a fine big man. He welcomed me warmly and after exchanging a few pleasantries we settled down at the fireside while Mary (we'll call her that) retreated to the kitchen to make tea. I took a deep breath and blurted out the news and then waited for the storm to break. There was no storm.

11

Paddy just sat there gazing into the fire for a few minutes in silence and then he spoke. "Well Father, if she had to look for a bit of loving from someone else then I must have been neglecting her. It's not the baby's fault. We'll keep it."

Mary must have been listening at the door.

She piped up: "But it'll have red hair."

"Hump the red hair," he said, "we'll keep it anyway."

There was nothing left for me to say.

I hugged him, she hugged him and we all hugged each other and the tragedy turned into a celebration and has continued as such to this day.

Paddy had been involved in so many clubs and committees that he now realised he had for years only eaten and slept in the house. He had provided all the necessary finance to make the home comfortable but nothing of himself. He knew his wife was a good woman and he knew that the flirtation was completely out of character and he blamed himself equally for it and accepted his share of the consequences.

His generosity was not lost on Mary. She saw him in a new light and the rest of the pregnancy was like a honeymoon for both of them. They are now, years later, one of the happiest couples I know. They have a fine son and he has since acquired a brother and sister. Incidentally he didn't have red hair—his hair is blonde.

I don't think there is any need for me to draw any conclusions from this story. I'll leave that to yourself.

True Love in Marriage

I've seen good young people come from bad homes and bad ones come from good homes but the odds are heavily in favour of the good ones coming from good homes and that of course means homes that are founded on happy and loving marriage relationships.

It's amazing how many good, hard-working couples miss out on the real joys of love because of their inability or shyness to express their feelings openly to each other. I know many solid quiet men who devote their whole lives to their families and love them with a fiercely protective love which only shows itself in what they do for them but can never express it in words and rarely in actions.

I know many women too, who lead lives of total dedication and self sacrifice but are afraid they might be deemed silly or flirtatious if they give verbal or physical expression to the love they feel within. People, in other words, don't tell each other that they love each other often enough and don't kiss and hug often enough and certainly can't discuss their physical desires and enjoy them fully enough in many good marriages that could be terrific and deservedly rewarding if those barriers were broken down.

So far I've talked about marriages where love exists but is not fully exploited. However, most of the marriage problems I get seriously question if love ever existed. Love impels us to give. In most breaking marriages the "love" appears to be a taking love—a desire to be loved rather than to love. When people demand their rights and almost keep accounts and measure what they get from each other, their love is very questionable. So often a husband or wife gives me a list of their spouse's imperfections and expect perfection that God Himself would not demand without adverting for one moment to their own greater imperfections.

Young people who will be potential parents rush into marriage after a glamorous courtship that confuses love with physical attraction and satisfaction and material comforts and good times. When the glitter goes and the pressures come and sacrifice is call for, their love emerges like the seeds that fell on rocky soil, as having very little depth or roots; it disappears very quickly with the help of misguided advice from equally ignorant friends.

Young people need to be educated on love and loving and need to take time off to think about it and how to cultivate it. They need to be able to recognise their own imperfections and to assess the perfections and imperfections of others and to weigh them carefully before making commitment to accept the whole package, good and bad.

They need time, preparation and education. That is why I oppose short courtships and teenage marriages in general and would like to see church and state provide the education and support and if necessary the compulsion required to insure that young love will become mature love and will have the roots strong enough to survive the many tests that life has in store for it.

Even the names given in baptism by young couples to their babies indicate that their knowledge of love is mainly learned from TV "soaps". They need to know the love that leads to happiness—the love that St. Paul tells us about.

Real love has strong roots. The soil in which these roots can develop is of course, firstly, the preparation and mature understanding of the people involved. These are the essential roots that will help them to cling tenaciously together in the worst of situations. The soil can be made more fertile and produce even stronger roots if the basic material requirements, particularly in regards to family income and accommodation, are available.

Ideally, security of employment and reasonable comforts can provide the wind-breakers that will give young love the chance to grow even stronger and become more deeply rooted with a reasonable freedom from early pressure.

It is important that young people should make proper material preparations for marriage. To do this, they need the opportunity as well as sound advice and guidance. The birds of the air build a nest before they mate and that is the logical and natural procedure but they do have the opportunity and materials to do it as well as the ability. Many young couples have the ability and willingness. They need the opportunity and they need encouragement and they get precious little of either.

The Right to a Happy Childhood

One day last Summer I spent a Sunday afternoon at Portmarnock. The sun was shining, the beach was crowded and everyone was happy. I sat listening to the shrieks and splashes and laughter of hundreds of children and watched them race from the water to the security and comfort of a mother's arms and a large towel.

I watched fathers, too, queuing for ice-cream or hot-water and shedding their own years as they played games and built castles as happily as any of the children. It was a lovely sight and I enjoyed it.

There was no thought of strikes, borders or budgets. Before me were people who loved each other and were happy to share God's good things with each other. I remember similar outings and days in my own childhood and I thank God for them.

I honestly believe that a happy and secure childhood is the necessary foundation on which an adult life that is to be in any way stable, fruitful, and caring, can be built. Those children on the beach before me will soon have to face the realities and hardships of life, but they will be all the better equipped for those happy childhood days and the love and time their parents now give them.

There is an element of the spoil-sport in my nature which comes to the surface just when I'm enjoying myself, so it wasn't long till I thought of the many children who don't get the chances of a happy or secure childhood that they are entitled to, and who are the ones most likely to swell the ranks of our drop-outs, misfits and problem people.

We adults are usually the authors of our own misfortunes but children are born innocent and have a right to the proper start in life which we call a happy childhood. If their parents can't or won't provide this start, then the obligation falls on all of us as relatives, neighbours, members of the community, and as Christians who care.

The birds of the air and indeed the whole animal kingdom give us a marvellous example of how to prepare our young for the life that lies ahead. Two birds will first build a secure nest and then proceed to have a family. When the chickens are hatched out the parents' main preoccupation is the feeding and protection of them, and then the training and preparation of them for their eventual and inevitable departure.

Many children are victims of their parent's irresponsibility in making no reasonable preparation for marriage and no reasonable effort to provide a home or "nest" in which the family can grow securely. Some are victims of selfish parents who bring them into the world and then, in pursuing their own selfish pleasures, find them a burden and abandon, desert, neglect and at times ill-treat them.

Others are victims of a community or state which does not give the material or moral support to good parents when circumstances beyond their control make it essential that they get some support. Whatever the causes of their problems those children are innocent victims and we all share responsibility for them.

Since the happy family home is the ideal and natural place for a child to develop, then on a national level the government must do everything to encourage and support family life through the provision of adequate housing and financial support and any other supportive services that can help.

At local levels, communities can do a lot to help in many neighbourly caring wars. I think immediately of local advice and home help services, summer projects, community games, playgrounds, baby sitting services etc. For people who have sick children or handicapped children, there is a need for the support that special schools and services can give: they are entitled to special consideration and help from the state and from each of us as individuals.

Organisations like the Wheelchair Association and St. Michael's House and schools like those run by the brothers of St. John of God do not absolve us from responsibility. They simply discharge a large part of it for us but can only do so with our generous and continued support.

At the bottom of the heap are children whose parents are incapable of caring for them. Usually some good neighbours and other members of the family take on the responsibility and do a marvellous job but this is not always possible. Such children become the responsibility of the state and the state needs the help of individuals to give them what no state can really give—warmth and love and a sense of belonging. Our health boards are always looking for foster parents and will always welcome enquiries.

Preparing Your Children for Marriage

I have often pleaded the cause of young couples, but I must in fairness say that many young couples are the authors of their own misfortune. Or perhaps I could even blame their parents . .

At a time when credit is tight, costs are rising, and everybody is feeling the pinch, one sector of the community is having a ball, namely, the irresponsible young single people. I say only the *irresponsible* because I have great admiration for the many *responsible* young people.

A single boy or girl taking home £70 to £90 per week, or even more, can have a marvellous time now if they don't care about the future. Give mother £10 per week and blow the rest on drink, gambling, cards, etc.

I have often written about our national drink bill. Each year our gambling records soar. Now a car has become a "must" in the lives of most young men.

All too often, young couples come to arrange their marriage without a penny saved. For them the good times are over as soon as they marry.

I appeal to parents, particularly, to encourage their young people to think in terms of their future long term before they consider getting engaged—indeed, long before they even begin courting.

Their training in thrift and savings should begin as children. As soon as they earn their first wages, certain decisions should be made. Apart from their contribution to the family budget, a substantial part of their earnings should be taken and saved for them and only released for requirements that are judged useful after mature discussion.

In other words, they must be trained to entertain and amuse themselves on much the same amount as they will have available in marriage. We cannot adjust our standards downwards and a young person accustomed to spending £50 per week on entertainment will look very ruefully at the few pounds left to him after his household commitments are met in marriage.

I find that mothers are generally too soft on their sons and do not prepare them for the sharing and caring that marriage involves. Where daughters are concerned, too, many mothers concentrate on a "good catch" and the wedding reception. Indeed, often they go so far overboard on the trimmings that they run the young couple into ridiculous expenses for cars, wedding albums, bridesmaids and outfits, pages, carnations and "whatever you're having yourself".

Keeping up with the Jones's has come to be the all-important consideration and I only wish people would realise that the Jones's would be delighted with a chance to draw a breath if only the other foolish people would stop chasing them.

The wedding day may be a great success socially, but it is probably the least important day in the whole marriage. Young people can be expected to get carried away with glamour and emotion. Parents should be the ones to see and point out the more practical aspects of their plans, and yet the most frustrating attitude I meet when I fight for postponements and preparation is that of the mother who says: "Ah but, Father, they love each other."

Parents, interfere now! When they are married, leave them alone. If you do interfere now, there won't be any need to do so later on—nor will you have the right.

The Blessing of
a Good Home

When June comes round every year my thoughts turn to the
thousands of young people who are enduring the pressures that
exams and the need for good results bring. They've already
been under some pressure and unfortunately there is much
more to come. The children who are not even equipped to
attempt exams have an even tougher road ahead.

When I think of the many pressures from all sides on young
people, I marvel that so many of them are so good. I thank God
that I had the chance of a longer period of childhood with less
pressures, because I just might not have survived. There is no
doubt that, materially, children are much better off now, but
this material well-being very often causes them problems, too.
Young people have money now, so the best brains in advertis-
ing and salesmanship use their experience and expertise to
extract that money from them without any regard as to how
their methods and products affect their moral and intellectual
development.

In my day, I could stroll through the Leaving Cert. and
decide afterwards about my career or vocation. Nowadays,
young people have to make decisions at 14 or 15 about their
future in order to take the right subjects and apply to the right
places, and even when they get the exam. they have no guarantee that they can continue on the course they have set themselves. Of course, there are greater opportunities for young
people to develop their full potential now if things go right for
them. However, unless they are motivated and equipped to

take advantage of these opportunities, they are headed for problems.

The potentially good have the chance to be very good and successful, but the potentially bad are assured of many helps and pulls to be bad. Drugs, drink, abuse of sex and violence, are all available and fashionable, and can only be handled by the youngster who is properly prepared for life with the wisdom to discern right from wrong and good from bad—and the courage to do what is right in spite of the pressures against it.

In fairness to the present generation of teenagers, I must say that in general they are more serious and more concerned about real problems than the generation before them. We read of vandalism, hooliganism and juvenile delinquency, but we don't read or hear nearly enough about the many young people who, in many diverse groups, projects and ways show a sincerity and concern about people and problems that I certainly didn't have at their age. I was interested in sports, films and girls mostly. Neither I nor my schoolmates gave much thought to old folks, charity walks, peace vigils, or prayer groups. I am constantly edified by the activities of many youth groups. Such youngsters make me optimistic about the future, in spite of the depressing headlines given to the minority of thugs and delinquents.

I don't propose here to go into all the causes of juvenile problems. I could begin by blaming the Government and work my way down through local councils, schools and broken marriages, but that wouldn't help anyone. What I do hope to do here is to make a few points that might be helpful to parents and others immediately responsible for the care of children.

Children are a great gift from God, but they are a great responsibility, too, and that responsibility belongs primarily to parents. The birds of the air prepare and train their young carefully to fly before they leave the nest and the good home is the ideal nest in which a young person should be prepared for life. The parents must always keep in mind that their children will some day have to leave the nest and that it is their duty to prepare them for that time, so that when it comes they are not just sitting ducks for every temptation, distraction and influence, but will be able to fly steadily and strongly on their set course against even the strongest winds.

The State, the Church, the school and other agencies can all help, but the most important single factor in the development of a youngster is a good home. Mind you, I've seen good children come form bad homes, and bad ones come from good homes, but the odds are that the good, successful and integrated child will come from the good home. All that parents can do is to increase the odds. They must do their best and leave the rest to God.

I sympathise fully with parents who do their best and are frustrated by outside influences, but the frustration should not prevent them from doing their best. When one or other parent fails or refuses to play their part the other is still expected by God to carry on. The same applies when housing conditions and other factors prevent parents from providing all that they would like to.

When young people get into difficulties or trouble, parents often feel guilty. They feel that they have failed, when in fact they shouldn't if they have done what they could with what they were given. Even Christ didn't do a perfect job with the 12 apostles. Two of them let him down at crucial moments! There must be a message of consolation there for parents who are given the care of a number of children. If you have six children and none of them put a foot wrong, then you are scoring better than Christ!

The purpose of a good home is to prepare children fully for life in the world they are going into and to help them to develop the ability and habit of thinking and making right judgments for themselves and the confidence and backbone to act on those judgments. The end-product should be a young person who knows what life is about and what he wants out of life; a youngster who has a goal in life which is important to him not just because his parents say so, but because with their help he has figured it out for himself and it has become a part of him. The child you are now preparing for Confirmation will in a few short years be a young adult in a flat in London or New York, or maybe a student in Dublin. You won't be there to tell him or her what to do or what not to do. They'll have to figure things out for themselves and if they haven't the habit, ability and self-confidence, they'll be in difficulties. If they're not equipped to "do their own thing", they'll be merely "puppets on a string" and there'll be plenty of wrong influences tugging at that string.

A good home is not necessarily a rich home or a poor home, nor do its physical dimensions matter, either. A good home for me is one that has the sort of atmosphere in which this "end-product" I talked about is most likely to grow.

The State Must Support Marriage

If I were to judge marriage and family life by the cases that come to my door I would be in despair. However, I have also seen many happy marriages and lovely homes and I realised long ago that the most common element that distinguishes the good from the bad is unselfish love.

Marriage is a life-time vocation. It is a very demanding commitment. It requires knowledge, skills, maturity and above all, true love. It is up to the parents, church and state, to ensure that those are present as far as possible before ever a young couple are allowed to marry. The only profession in which written exams and qualifications are not required is that of a jockey. For bricklaying and plumbing, etc., examination certificates are required. A jockey at least has to spend time learning his business. As things stand however, any two sub-normal children can present themselves for marriage according to the state and no one can refuse them or even delay them in their purpose.

I meet all kinds of couples. Some I'm happy about and others I'm not. Some are too young. They love each other in a superficial way. They have no savings, no accommodation, none of the skills of housekeeping or management and their main concern is the reception, the ceremony, and the honeymoon. They blissfully think that everything else will follow smoothly from there. They'll live with the Mammy or get a flat, put their names down for a corporation house and live on the dole. They won't contemplate the pressures of crowded living or conflicts of temperament or pregnancy, or children or the fact that they could be four or five years waiting for a house, which will then be too late. They've read a lot of true romance stories and they won't even do a pre-marriage course because they "want to find out for ourselves." They are at the bottom of the scale. They haven't a chance and they will become a burden on themselves, their families and society.

There are others who are old enough and have good jobs, but as single people have spent every penny on living it up. They get used to cars, Chinese takeaways, and vodka and tonic, and the shock of paying rent or mortgage on one salary and doing without a car and their drinking sessions is too much for them. I blame the parents mostly for this.

There are many great young couples who prepare spiritually and materially and grow closer together in doing so, but even they need great courage and patience and unselfish love if they are to overcome together the obstacles that lie in their way. First, there is the tremendous expense of the reception which their families expect them to lay on. Then there is the question of a house. Prices keep going up. Savings can't keep pace with inflation. Mortgages are difficult to obtain and there are all kinds of extras such as legal fees and surveyors' fees for bankers and building societies. Unnecessary delays involve expensive bridging loans. A Corporation or Co. Council loan is obtained, but it is never enough and so a crippling second loan must be sought if it can be got at all. When the Co. Council loan was £7,000, couples needed £10,000. When it went to £9,000, they needed £12,000, and so it goes . . . it is the extra couple of thousand that causes problems. If they wait to save it, the price will have jumped but the maximum loan won't, and so they are still in trouble.

A further pressure on young couples is the fact they very often have to live in new estates that are far from the town, their work and their relatives. Add the present problems of unemployment, recession and high taxation and you see that there is a multitude of pressures on the very best of marriages.

If the pressures get too great and if they begin to tear each other apart rather than support each other, then divorce is not the answer. They need positive help, guidance and encouragement which at present is available in a very flimsy way from the churches and not at all from the State.

The State must increase its support for marriages in the schools, educating children in relationships and providing them with the knowledge and skills required for parenthood. It must set minimum requirements of preparation and notice for marriage. It must look at its housing and loan programmes.

The State must cut away a lot of the red tape and extra expenses of house purchase. It must provide, or subsidise, proper positive counselling services and it must provide proper marriage tribunals to take marriage disputes away from the cold, legalistic atmosphere of the present courts.

Staying Single Can Be a Vocation Too

When we speak of vocations, we usually have the priesthood or religious life in mind. We extend that sometimes to a profession or trade or to marriage or parenthood. The only vocation I never hear much talk about is the vocation of the single life.

Apart from priests and those bound by a vow of celibacy I believe that there are many single lay people who are called to remain single by God because they have key roles to play in His plan of creation.

I know many single people who feel, or are made to feel by others, almost apologetic for the fact that they have not married. It's almost as if they have failed in life. For a single woman, the "old maid" or "left on the shelf" tags are inevitable, and indicate an attitude in society that is blind to the necessary and vital part that single people have to play in life.

While I believe that there is a place for married clergy in the church I also strongly believe that there will always be a need for a celibate clergy too. The ties and responsibilities of marriage would be incompatible with the freedom and mobility required for a full exercise of the priesthood in many cases. The same applies to lay people. For the vast majority the married state is their vocation and is indeed conducive to a full contribution to society of their talents and skills. A minority, however, are called by God to give of themselves totally, in a way they could not if they were married.

Some single people never get the opportunity to marry. Most do get it, but pass it up for one reason or another. Others get it but decline it for unselfish and sometimes quite heroic reasons.

I know single people who believe their work is so important that it demands their total attention. Either it would be impeded by marriage or the marriage would be impeded by the work. I know others who, because of some personal problem or infirmity, feel that they would place unfair burdens on a spouse. I know also many fine people who gave up their right to a happy marriage because of their responsibilities to aged parents or younger or infirm brothers and sisters.

The saddest aspect of single life is that single people are not sufficiently appreciated for the contribution they make to society. They will be joked about, sneered at, envied sometimes but very seldom appreciated or considered. Indeed, if any praise is given to the work of a single person the most common reaction is: "It's all right for him, he has no responsibilities."

I have met many fine women who have given their lives to a school or hospital or family or some other job with a devotion and fullness that would have been impossible if they were married. Old age doesn't hold many inviting prospects for them. Within a few years they are forgotten people in the very places they gave their lives to.

As John Donne said: "No man is an island." It is a part of our nature to want to be loved and appreciated. The single life is a lonely life. The bachelor or spinster who may be important at work returns to an empty flat and a lonely bed and eventually retires without children or grandchildren to support and love them. Far from being objects of derision or envy, most single people I know are to be admired and cherished.

As a priest, I come in contact with many aspects of life. Voluntary bodies like the Legion of Mary and Vincent de Paul Society, essential social groups, drama groups, youth clubs and even golf clubs, hospitals and other institutions, schools and universities—all of them operate smoothly and efficiently only because somewhere among their personnel is a single person who provides the continuity and dedication of one married to the job.

Perhaps the most tragic effect of our ignorant attitudes to unmarried adults is the number of people who become real failures by making unsuitable marriages rather than be "left on the shelf".

Single people play a vital role at all levels of society. We need them and can only repay them by embracing them into our own family life. As a single person myself, I know the strength and warmth I get from the affection of my sisters and nieces and nephews. It helps me to do my work better and removes my fears of a lonely old age. I know of course that I have a contribution to make in my role as a brother or uncle too. It is a two-way thing, with benefits to all concerned.

The Magic of Christmas

Christmas for me is above all else a family time. Of course, that's what it should be, since it commemorates the beginning of the Holy Family. Many aspects of Christmas have changed for me over the years but the one constant factor has been that I have always eaten my Christmas dinner in my family home, even though some of the chairs that used to be filled are empty now or occupied by new faces.

As a child, Christmas was pure magic. Living in the city in a public-house near the markets, I found my mornings beginning to the babble of turkeys, geese and quacking ducks and I dodged my way to school through horse-drawn carts filled with cabbage, brussels sprouts, and all the other farm products that make up the peculiar smell of the Dublin markets.

When the war ended, Fyffes bananas and the big Jaffa oranges appeared and I also saw my first pineapples. I made myself very busy, running in and out of the shop on imaginary messages and invariably got a few pence from jovial customers who were celebrating the sale of their goods.

Christmas always began for me with the making of the puddings, which was a family ritual. My sisters did the breadcrumbs while I was kept on the run for more candied peel or stout, or whatever additional ingredients were required. When Santa stopped coming to me, something big that could never be replaced went out of Christmas for me. The thrill of waking at an unearthly hour to find parcels all over the room and the rush and jump on to my parents' bed has never been adequately replaced in my life.

We always dined in the kitchen but Christmas dinner had to be eaten in the diningroom. I suppose every family has its own traditions and we had ours—it was we, the children, who insisted on lemonade. No other mineral would do, and it had to be in siphons from which the glasses could be filled with fuzzy froth. The siphons are gone, but to this day I always have lemonade with my Christmas dinner.

Christmas did not end with the dinner. Our home was the focal point where all the friends and relations gathered that night for laughter, games, singing and storytelling. Everyone did their party piece and it was usually the same song or recitation each year. We would be disappointed if it wasn't!

Christmas is a totally happy time for children. For adults, it is a time for looking back with wistful and nostalgic memories at Christmases gone by. My Christmases were childlike till my mother died. I became an adult them. With all due respect to my father and all fathers, the mother is usually the heart of the home and when she goes, home and Christmas just aren't the same. Nobody cooks the turkey or makes a pudding like your mother; they just don't taste the same.

I am fortunate that I have never missed a Christmas at home and I still enjoy and look forward to it very much. My preparation is different now. My satisfaction comes from the huge number at confession, the family groups at communion, and the general goodwill and generosity that I witness all round.

My celebration of it is different, too. I obviously have a deeper spiritual appreciation of its significance. Midnight Mass is now my high point. Material gifts no longer mean much to me. I sometimes feel like someone who has had his Christmases and wants others to have the same and gets his enjoyment out of helping them to do so. I look back at the past and the memories don't sadden me. I relive them and feed off them and thank God for them. I feel sorry for those who haven't such memories.

My memories are of people, of love, of laughter and good cheer. Those are the ones we should try to provide our children with. I enjoy watching my nieces listening to stories, and recalling the past. The parcels and gifts are left to one side as they sit well-filled and wide-eyed around the fire, enthralled and forgetful of time as I so often was many years ago. Children may seem more sophisticated now, but they are still children and they go through the same stages of childhood and have the same needs. Of course, we should give them presents but we should also give them the things that will last longer after the presents are gone and forgotten—the love, the joy, the laughter and the stories that will provide them with lasting memories to feed off for the years ahead.

Christmas for me is still a happy time and still a family time. Christmas has not changed, but it is the part I play in it that has changed. I am no longer a child receiving: I am an adult giving. I enjoyed a long spell of childhood, but I now equally enjoy my role as an adult. I have no time for those who say they no longer enjoy Christmas. If they adapt to their new role they will find as much enjoyment out of adult giving as they did out of childhood receiving.

At Christmas I thank God for that first Christmas and what it meant to mankind. I thank God for my childhood and family. I pray for my parents, and friends and relations who left me such happy memories and I sit down with my sisters and nieces not in sadness but joyfully to play my part as an uncle to contribute to their future memories. I pray that they will be as happy as mine.

Lent Can Make Your Life Better

Lent is a time of penance. Traditionally we prepare for the biggest feast of the year by introducing some self-imposed discipline into our lives.

Penance, however, presupposes genuine feeling and sorrow for our past failings. It is the sign of our desire to make up for our many offences against God's love. Our self-imposed penances would be meaningless, if we were not aware of our faults and sorry for them, and had not already made things right with God. For a Catholic, this means that we must already enjoy a clear friendship with Christ or re-establish it through the Sacrament of Penance.

Lent is a great time for parish retreats and ample opportunities are afforded for those who wish to make a sincere Confession of their sins and enjoy the reassuring certainty of an absolution given by Christ's representative and in His name. There are just a few points I would like to make about Confession.

There is no sin that God won't forgive. The essential requirement is that we have the desire to love God and with His help to continue in His love. There is no limit to the number of times we can seek his forgiveness. His love and mercy are foolish, so let us be glad of that and make use of it. It doesn't matter how often we fall. The important thing is to keep getting up, as Christ did on His way to Calvary. Peter got up and became the first Pope. Poor Judas lay down. He mistrusted the infinity of God's mercy, very much as people do when they

34

day: "Ah, you'd never forgive me father", or: "The priest would kill me."

Some people with habitual sins feel they must conquer the habit or problem first before they can go to Confession. They may never succeed alone, but with the regular use of the sacrament they can eventually win out.

Shame is another barrier that should not keep anyone from God's friendship. Whoever else you may shock, you should not be able to shock a confessor. He has heard it all before and knowing the vagaries of human nature and human responses, he expects the best from the worst and the worst from the best. I could honestly put a sign up "£100 reward for a new sin" without any fear of losing money!

Fear is a barrier that I must admit is contributed to by some priests. No priest should be nasty or cynical or sarcastic or angry when representing Christ in Confession. Unfortunately priests are human too and we've all heard of people being "bawled out" or "thrown out", though the stories do tend to be exaggerated out of proportion.

Some people give up Confession—even all practice of their faith—because of this. Mind you, the same people wouldn't give up drink just because they met a nasty barman! If you want Christ's love and friendship badly enough, you won't let any grumpy priest keep you away from Him. My advice is to get up, say "Good luck, Father, I'll pray for your arthritis," and go to another priest. The vast majority of priests feel only privileged at being the instrument of re-uniting the Good Shepherd with one of His lost sheep.

What about sorrow and purpose of amendment? Christ knew the sort of people we were and that's why He gave us the sacrament to be used time and again. We can't say we didn't enjoy what we did or guarantee that we won't do it again, but we can be sorry that in enjoying ourselves we offended God and we can sincerely ask for His help in resisting or avoiding such occasions again. The little boy who has a few licks at the cream and generally messes up the cake his mother had for the visitors can't say "Ma, I didn't enjoy it". He can say "Ma, I'm sorry I've upset you" and he can say too "Ma, don't leave it there again."

Above all, don't judge yourself or listen to others who may advise you strongly. Whatever your sin or problem or apparently hopeless situation you find yourself in, go to Confession anyway. You won't come away unhappy. Things that may be objectively wrong in themselves may not involve serious guilt in the circumstances in which they happen. Killing is always a bad thing and yet circumstances in each individual case can make the killer guilty of murder or manslaughter or guilty of no sin at all.

Remember also that there is no sin too big for God to forgive. If you want God's love you can't be kept from it, but you can be helped towards it and restored to it in the Sacrament of Penance.

Make a good Confession as part of your preparation for Easter. Don't wait till Holy Week. Do it as early as you can in Lint and give the rest of the Lenten exercises real penitential value and meaning.

Easter Sunday is a Day of Rejoicing

Easter Sunday is the day on which we should celebrate and rejoice more than any other day in the year. It is the anniversary of the greatest event in the history of mankind. It is the day on which Christ made life worth living and filled it with new hope and purpose for every man. It is the day on which He gave man eternal life.

Death for the unbeliever is a bleak and frightening and futile ending. It is something he dreads to think about or refuses to contemplate. He can only look at it as an oblivion, sometimes preferable to a miserable or pointless life.

For the Christian, the Resurrection give a whole new meaning to death and makes it something to live for. Christ conquered death once for all. Death is no longer a meaningless ending but a very meaningful beginning. For the true Christian, life is a period of courtship leading to a loving union with God which is sealed for eternity by that irrevocable step we call death.

Saintly people look forward to death and pray for it and the happiness it brings. In doing so they get the bonus of a happy earthly life too, because their faith and anticipation make the pains of this life tolerable, worthwhile, useful and meaningful.

On that first Easter Sunday there wasn't much joy. The apostles and disciples were in despair and perhaps a little ashamed of their own cowardice. Their faith was wavering and it took the calm strength of Mary to keep it alive. Even when the rumour of the Resurrection began to spread, there was incredulity and, at best, wild hope. We have the benefit of hindsight. We know the whole story, so we have every reason to celebrate with great faith and great hope.

I always look forward to the brightness of Easter. The white vestments, the candles, the flowers, the singing, dispel the gloom of Lent and even the weather seems to brighten and give the promise of summer. The daffodils and primroses make their contribution to the scene also. I suppose I wouldn't really enjoy their freshness and newness fully if I hadn't experienced winter and lived out the penitential season of Lent.

Easter Sunday can only be fully appreciated and enjoyed by someone who has lived out the preceding days of Holy Week. The story of Christ is the greatest love story ever told and Holy Week is its high point. To live through Holy Week with Christ is a renewal of faith and love. It couldn't have any other effect. If you refuse to participate in the ceremonies of Holy Week then I'm sorry for you: you don't know what you are missing and you must ask yourself seriously what Christ really means to you.

The events of the Passion show us vividly the love of Christ for us. His suffering and pain were very real and His Divine Sonship did not diminish them one bit. His desire for support when he asked "could you not watch one hour with me", his human plea to the Father to "take away this Chalice", his simple words on the cross, "I thirst", and his agonised cry, "My God, my God, why have you abandoned me," all indicate the price he paid for his love of you and me.

We can excuse the terror and cowardice and lack of strength in those who should have supported him then, but we cannot excuse ourselves. In Holy Week we have an opportunity to make some return for his love. We were there when they crucified our Lord. We were there through our sins to join the soldiers in pressing on the crown of thorns and wielding the whips and hammering in the nails.

Now we can change sides. We can watch that hour with him, as we acknowledge him; we can accompany him and carry his cross, we can wipe his brow and we can give him the comfort of knowing that it was all worthwhile. Only then can we really celebrate the resurrection with a full appreciation of what our Redemption really cost.

One of my most abiding images of Christ in his sufferings is that of the Crucified Saviour hanging on the cross still able to look with love and understanding at the men who had just put him there and pleading with a foolish excuse: "Father forgive them for they know not what they do".

I was one of "them" and you were one of "them", and that's the kind of love Christ has for us and it's the kind of love he wishes us to have for each other.

The Grace of the Sacraments

The celebration of Holy Week and Easter reminds us of what Christ did for us. He redeemed us, he gave life a new meaning and a new dimension. He re-opened heaven to us. This does not mean, however, that we all, as a consequence, will go to heaven or must go to heaven. He did not remove our free will. We are still free to be good or bad—to choose God or not.

Christ played His part but we have to play our part too. We are totally free to make our own choice. We must have faith, but faith alone is not enough. We must choose God and love Him and emphasise our choice and prove our love by the way we live our lives.

This isn't easy. There will always be a struggle in our lives between the forces of good and evil. The weaknesses of human nature will always be a handicap. The attractions of worldly success or pleasure will often obscure our real worthwhile and lasting goal and divert or distract us from it. Christ knew this and so he didn't simply do the job his Father sent him to do.

He gave us many helps to keep us on course for salvation. He gave them to us because he knew we would need them. It is important that we realise their need and availability and that we use them. We will only use them fully and effectively if we know what they are and what they have to offer us and are seriously concerned about our salvation.

Christ gave us a Church to teach and guide and minister to us. He gave us the example of his own life and his teaching through the Scriptures. He taught us how to pray. He promised us the help of the Holy Spirit and, in a last desperate desire to do something more for us while hanging on the Cross, he gave us his mother to be our mother and intercessor.

When Jesus died on the Cross he paid an infinite price for an inexhaustible flow of grace which would enable each man to overcome obstacles and to remain united with God through eternity.

The means he chose through which to channel this grace was the sacraments. He could have used some other means, but he chose to deal with man in this matter of grace in the same way in which he had made man—through a union or combination of the physical and spiritual, of body and soul. The grace itself would be invisible but it would come to us through the visible things with which we deal daily.

God took things of this world that we can touch , feel, and taste. He added words that we could hear and gestures that we could understand and he made these the vehicles of his grace. He even chose the objects to indicate the purpose for which the grace was given. He used water for the grace that cleanses, bread and wine for the grace that nourishes and oil for the grace that heals and strengthens.

A simple definition of a sacrament is an outward sign instituted by Christ to give grace. The "outward sign" is the material or thing used as, for example, water in baptism. It is completed by the words used which specify or give meaning to what we are doing. The water in baptism is called the "matter" and the words "I baptise thee" are the "form" which gives meaning to the actions.

We know that no human power could attach an inward grace to an outward sign and so a key element in the definition of a sacrament is that it is instituted by Christ. The Church cannot institute new sacraments. We use various sacramentals as spiritual aids but they cannot compare with and should never be place above those aids which have the stamp of Jesus Christ himself on them.

The third element in our definition is the purpose "to give

grace". The sacrament gives grace of itself. It is not dependent on the moral fitness of the minister. Provided the correct matter is used, with the correct form and with the correct intention by someone validly empowered to do so, the sacrament gives grace of itself, because Christ has guaranteed it.

Prayers, novenas and relics are all useful and commendable, but none of them carry the certainty of effective help that the sacraments do through their institution by Christ. The tragedy is that, through lack of knowledge or awareness, we do not make full use of these great gifts and do not use them to the best effect.

The sacrament of the sick is a perfect example of a sacrament that is not used to full effect and with full understanding. We say we believe that this is a sacrament carrying Christ's guarantee of spiritual and physical help at a time when we have a special need for such help. That's what we *say* we believe, but our poor use or even avoidance of it indicates a weak faith or a poor understanding of the sacrament.

Sick people will use medals, relics, holy water and everything else except the sacrament which carries the surest help of all. Very rarely does anyone ask straight out for this sacrament. All too often it is administered when the patient is past consciousness, because relatives delay calling the priest in case "he might frighten him".

Apart from the recent trend of administering the sacrament of the sick to groups at special masses for the sick, most priests will tell you that of all the people they anointed, most were unaware of what was happening or had to be "conned" to some extent. I myself have often been called to a sick person hours later than I should have been and somewhere in the middle of the night I'm expected to pretend I was "just passing".

I'll never forget one occasion when a lady asked me outside the church one day if I would call to her house to anoint her. My surprise was so obvious that she said: "I've got cancer, I've about three months to live. Am I not entitled to it?"

I replied: "Of course you are, but you are the first person who ever asked me straight out for it."

I'll always remember her reply. "Father, I know I'm dying and I want to use every help I can get to die well."

For the first time ever I administered the sacrament as it should be—joyously and openly.

Heard Anything About Sin Lately?

Have you heard anything about sin or hell lately? I'm taking a risk even mentioning them here now. They are dirty words belonging to the past and must not be used in this enlightened age. It's alright to discuss sex and abortion and divorce and breast feeding and other such matters on radio and television but you mustn't upset people by telling them that sin and hell still exist and are very real matters for consideration.

Sin is an offence against the love of God. It is the title we give to any contravention of God's command to "love the Lord your God and your neighbour as yourself". There is no doubt that this commandment is broken daily by most of us and so sin is still very much in.

I'm not too worried by the fact that people fight shy of using the term "sin" for their failures and misdemeanours but I am worried that so many people seem to have lost all sense of sin and all fear of its consequences.

Perhaps in the past we were too fearful of God and too sensitive and worried about keeping the letter of His laws. Obviously it's better to serve God out of love than fear, and we should not be worried about petty pernickety little human errors or failings, but it's my experience that people either forget God in their selfishness or ignore their responsibilities to Him on the presumption that His love will not allow Him to implement His justice.

Frequently people say to me: "Sure if God loves us that much there couldn't be a Hell."

The mistake they make, of course, is that God doesn't send

44

us to hell. We head for it ourselves with every step we take away from God. The punishment of hell is the permanent absence of God. In this sense, for some people, their hell can begin on earth. God never rejects us: we reject Him. We do so when we pursue our own selfish desires. His love is always reaching out to us, but we turn our love inwards on ourselves.

In any human love affair there is need for mutual loving and there is a need for regular contact and communication to keep the affair alive and growing. When communication stops and the loving weakens there is a breaking point where the affair ends and the love may even turn sour and bitter and vindictive. God differs from all other lovers in that His love never ends and never turns sour and is never vindictive. At any time we can turn back to Him.

If we end up in hell it is because we have chosen to do so.

As I already said, sin is when we hurt God and particularly when we do this through hurting other people. Our self-love can become so all-consuming that we can blind ourselves and justify and excuse ourselves as we satisfy and boost our egos at the expense of others.

Every love affair brings pain and sacrifice as well as pleasure and security. Many people make the mistake of thinking they can have the comfort of God's love without making the sacrifices or accepting the crosses that go with it. So many of us who got our religion easy wear our faith like a comfortable coat we inherited, but when it begins to pinch a little we can quite easily tear holes in it or discard it. It should be a part of ourselves, like our skin, that we won't tear and cannot discard if it is to be the sort of faith that feels and shares not only the joys of God's love but also His pain and suffering.

Nobody steals or cheats or kills anymore. Nowadays we have perks and mixers, and justified violence and numerous practices known as "good business". Mind you, we still call those activities by their proper names when they are carried out by others and particularly when we are the victims, but we

45

ourselves never commit sin because we have no obligations any longer, only rights.

Our churches are as full as ever and the numbers receiving Communion are increasing. It's no wonder that many of our young people are turned off religion when among the most pious-looking people in the church they see the woman who deplores vandalism but buys stolen property from the vandals, the worker who regularly brings home goods from his place of employment, the employer who pays unchristian wages (maybe even the parish priest!) or the farmer who fiddled the cattle cards, the speculator who fiddled planning permission, the painter who charged for three coats of paint where he put one, the mechanic who charges double time for his work and the many others who, without breaking the civil law or indeed by skilful manipulation and use of it, are daily inflicting grave injustices on the aged, the helpless and the ignorant.

"As long as you did it to one of my least brethren you did it to me."

These are the very clear words of Christ and in judging us he won't pay too much attention to the niceties of the civil law. What counts with Christ is the hurt we cause or the good we do and the motives or malice that accompany it. You can be a respectable citizen in the eyes of the law and a sinner in the eyes of God.

When we criticise the government, the legal system, or inequality and injustice or even fight for the rights of others we must remember Christ's warning about first taking the plank out of our own eye before trying to remove the mote from someone else's eye. Justice and love begin with me, ultimately I am only responsible for the justice and love I give. Others are responsible for what I get. Our care and concern for others can of course lead us to campaign politically and socially for them, but we must begin with an honest look at our own conscience.

It is one thing to march self-righteously at the head of a

46

protest march or indeed to write self-righteously in a newspaper column. It is a different thing to look into our own hearts and try to see what God sees there. It could be an unpleasant sight and it might call for immediate remedial treatment—the kind that is still available in Confession. It is only when Christ is living fully and healthily again in my own soul that I can be of much use to others, and need have no fear of hell.

Giving Honour To God

The First Commandment obliges us to recognise and honour God. Like all the other Commandments, it is merely a direction to do what we should want to do anyway if we have a real knowledge, appreciation and love of God. It brings us His guaranteed promise of reciprocal love and happiness for ourselves.

In other words, we do ourselves a favour when we comply with this commandment. We honour God, firstly, by acts of faith. When we make an act of faith in the truths revealed by God we pay Him the highest compliment because we accept them simply on His word or say-so.

Of course, to do this we must know what God has revealed, realising He had some good reason for giving us those truths. We are obliged then to seek out and try to understand those truths in order to give our assent to them. In doing so we gain knowledge designed by God to help us to greater fulfilment and happiness. It's amazing how many people go through life relying purely on what scraps of knowledge they learned and now remember from their school-days. We go out of our way to improve our knowledge of the world and its ways and our jobs, hobbies, and interests but when we need God and seek Him our vague school-day memories leave us groping in the dark.

The most important thing in life for us is our relationship with God. To develop it we need to listen to sermons, read periodicals, join discussion groups and use any other available means to develop an adult understanding of God's truths that will give real meaning and direction to our lives. Of course, if we love God this will be a labour of love and no burden. It is

48

not enough to make an internal act of faith in God. The first Commandment obliges us also to make outward profession of our faith at times. We must never deny our faith or remain silent when silence is the equivalent of denial. We must not be ashamed of God. We should not wait till a choice is forced on us, but should proudly proclaim by our actions and words that we are what we are—believers and children of God.

Very few of us will ever be called to be heroic in the proclamation of our faith, but in smaller ways, like attendance at Mass and other liturgical functions, blessing ourselves passing a church, grace at meals, the Angelus and in many other ways we give witness to God and example and courage to others whose faith is weaker.

The biggest way in which we offend against faith is by apostasty. A lax Catholic is one who through carelessness and laziness does not practise his religion and thereby allows his faith to weaken. An apostate is a person who deliberately abandons his faith.

Brendan Behan used to say: "I'm a bad Catholic". He didn't abandon his faith. He simply admitted that he didn't practise it as well as he felt he should. There are many people like this. If you have a faith, you can't simply get it out of your system, but you can deny and abandon it publicly: this is apostasy.

Apostasy is a deliberate rejection and is usually done for marriage, material gain or personal promotion. It can also arise from laxity, whereby faith is gradually lost and then abandoned.

Heresy is another grave offence against faith, but it is not a total rejection. It is a rejection of some particular truth revealed by God and taught by the Catholic Church and of course is a major step towards apostasy because if God can be wrong on one point there is no particular reason for believing God on any point. Intellectual pride is very often the cause of heresy. A little knowledge can be a dangerous thing and some people become so puffed up with their knowledge that they no longer accept anything they don't know or can't understand. They become too proud to accept things on faith in God's word.

In these days of ecumenism, it is easy to slip into the heresy of indifferentism by holding that all religions are equally pleasing to God. Truth and error cannot be equally pleasing to God. Of course, we respect the sincerity of other religions and we believe that ultimately the important thing is that a person in good faith should serve God to the best of his ability according to his conscience. For this reason we attend other religious services such as funerals and weddings, but we must not attend them on a regular basis with the attitude that one is as good as another and any one will do.

We honour God by acts of faith, accepting truths we don't understand or couldn't have found out by ourselves precisely because He has revealed them. We have an obligation to study them and learn all we can about them. The greatest dangers to our faith are ignorance, carelessness and laxity of practice and the total loss or rejection of faith through our own fault is apostasy.

Keep Holy The Sabbath

The natural law demands that we acknowledge our dependence on God, and thank and adore God for His goodness to us.

With the hustle and bustle of daily life it is not possible for the average person to maintain all the time a conscious state of adoration and so it is obvious that we need to set aside a definite time for the fulfilment of this necessary and desirable duty.

From this it follows quite logically that we should have a special day reserved for worship of the Lord. Hence the Third Commandment—"Remember thou keep holy the Lord's Day."

In the Old Testament the Lord's Day was the Sabbath Day—the last day of the week. The early Christian Church changed this to the first day of the week—Sunday—because that day had been made specially holy to Christians by the events of Easter Sunday and Pentecost Sunday.

The change was probably also made to emphasise that the Old Testament preparation for the coming of the Messiah was over, and that God's final plan for the salvation of the world had begun. Nothing is said in the Bible about this change. We know of it only from the tradition of the Church. It is curious, therefore, that non-Catholics who say they believe nothing unless they can find it in the Bible nevertheless keep Sunday as the Lord's Day on the say-so of the Catholic Church.

The Third Commandment forbids all unnecessary servile work on Sunday and commands us to worship God in a special way on that day. I don't think that there is much need for me to discuss servile work, so I'll confine myself to the positive obligation to worship God.

For Catholics, the Church lays down the obligation to attend

Sunday Mass. The Mass is the great central act of worship of the Catholic Church. It is the renewal and reminder of Christ's sacrifice and God's love, and it is the great source of all graces for us. Our attendance at Mass must be physical and mental. We must be a part of the congregation and we must make a conscious effort to participate.

Most Catholics do attend Mass regularly, but many attend out of a sense of duty and others out of fear, while others attend only when they "feel" like it. It is important that we examine our whole attitude to Mass and our attendance at it.

So many people say that the Mass bores them, or that they get nothing out of it that it is important to point out that the Mass is God's celebration and not ours. While we should get something out of it, our primary purpose should be to put something into it—to give of ourselves, our time, and our love to God, and it is then that we are more likely to get something out of it.

I go to Mass for a number of reasons. Firstly, I go to honour my great lover and to show my love to the world by my very presence just as I attend my sisters' weddings without questioning whether they would be boring or entertaining but primarily to show my support and to contribute what I could to the happiness of the occasions.

Secondly, I go to Mass in response to the dying wish of my greatest friend, Jesus Christ, who said at the Last Supper: "Do this in memory of me."

I also go to hear the word of God and to learn more about Him and His will for me. When we love someone, we try to learn all we can about them and we don't tear up their letters. We keep them and re-read them in case we might have missed any important little detail. For most people once they have left school the only opportunity they have of hearing the word of God is at Sunday Mass.

Another reason why I go to Mass is to offer a gift to God. When the priest raises the chalice and paten, I reach up and pop in my own aches and pains and love, and offer them humbly for what they are worth to God, Who loves me so much and has done so much for me.

Another highlight of my attendance at Mass is the Communion. When we love someone it is natural to want to express that love in a physical way. The greatest physical expression of love between two people occurs when they join their bodies in married love and produce life. In Communion I receive the physical body of Christ into my body. I form a union with Christ, the end product of which should be spiritual life.

These are some of my reasons for going to Mass. What are yours? Can you really say that Mass bores you or that you get nothing out of it? Would it be more honest to say that you never really bothered to think about it or to try to understand what the Mass really is? Can you blame anyone for interpreting your deliberate absence on Sunday as anything other than a deliberate rejection of God and a sin more cold-blooded and inexcusable than any other sin committed in passion or in temper, or for some apparently gainful motive?

Why We Should Not Kill

The Fifth Commandment tells us clearly: "Thou shalt not kill."

This commandment refers to human life. The killing of animals is not an offence against this commandment though unnecessary or wanton killing or cruelty to animals is an abuse of God's gifts and as such is sinful.

The fact that all human life belongs to God is so obvious that everyone accepts that murder is wrong.

The areas that cause controversy are those which involve the killing of somebody for an apparently good reason. The easy guideline to solving those questions is that the only time when life may lawfully be taken is when it is necessary as a defence against an unjust aggressor. The aggression must be unjust and it must be of such a proportion and gravity that a necessary and adequate defensive action includes the possibility of killing.

Abortion and euthanasia cannot be justified on these grounds, as an unborn child or a dying person cannot be considered as an unjust aggressor: even if they are a cause of misery or embarrassment, or even a threat to our lives, we are never justified in taking life for those reasons. Unjust aggression is the only possible justification for killing and even then it should be avoided if at all possible.

What about capital punishment? Basically, capital punishment is an extension of the principle of self-defence. A lawful government has the duty to protect citizens against unjust attacks and sometimes, after a fair trial, claims the right to take the life of a convicted person in certain circumstances. Not everybody is happy that such a right exists, hence the worldwide differences of opinion and the fact that some countries no longer claim the right.

The Church does not encourage capital punishment, but at present permits it and leaves it to governments to decide for themselves how necessary it is.

The principle of self-defence extends to nations as well as to individuals. At times, soldiers may have to kill in the service of their countries when fighting a just war. The difficulty here is to establish when a war is a just one, if indeed there is any such thing. Briefly, a war may be considered a just one when a nation has to defend its right in a grave matter, when all other peaceful and reasonable methods of resolving the dispute have been tried. Such a war, to be just, must be carried out in accordance with the dictates of the natural law and international law, and it must not be prolonged any more than is necessary.

Even in a just war it is possible to sin by using unjust means. Some of our paramilitary organisations try to justify their activities on the grounds that they are fighting a just war, but they obviously do not fulfil the above conditions. Bombing innocent civilians and kangaroo courts, murders and knee-cappings, would be considered unjust means even in a just war.

Even our own life is not our own. It belongs to God and so we are accountable to Him for it. Far from being allowed to end our own life by suicide, we have each got the positive obligation to take reasonable care of our lives and bodies as well as those of our neighbours. Fighting, reckless or drunken driving, or any carelessness or deliberate omissions that might endanger life are grave offences against the Fifth Commandment. Such offences are obvious, but I wonder how many careless electricians, mechanics, or builders will allow themselves to think that they may be committing grave sin by their carelessness.

Apart from avoiding the risk of injury or loss of life, we have the further obligation to take reasonable care of our health. This doesn't mean we have to become hypochondriacs, but we must make reasonable use of medical help and behave responsibly when there is a risk of communicating disease to others. Since the life of the whole body is more important than any of its parts, it may be necessary at times to remove certain organs or amputate certain parts but again that may only be done when that part of the body becomes a threat to the life of the whole body. It is wrong, however, to mutilate the body unnecessarily and this would include sterilisation for its own sake.

Finally, this commandment obliges us to do our best to control ourselves emotionally. We should avoid broodings that will give rise to anger and hatred that will trigger off our hot temper. From experience, we must know our own reactions and so it is not enough to say: "I lost the oul head," or "I've a filthy temper". If I have a wicked dog, I must take extra steps to control it, and likewise with my own emotions: I must know this and take sufficient steps to control them.

The Abuse of Sex

For the purpose of this article, I'm going to group together the Sixth and Ninth Commandments, "Thou shalt not commit adultery" and "Thou shalt not covet thy neighbour's wife."

Each Commandment mentions specifically one of the most serious sins against the virtue to be practised, and under that heading we group all the duties and sins of the allied nature.

Thus, not only is it a sin to commit adultery, but it is also a sin to indulge in any deliberate actions for the purpose of arousing the sexual appetite outside of marriage. Not only is it a sin to covet your neighbour's wife, but it is also wrong to willingly entertain unchaste thoughts or desires concerning any person. Objectively then, all deliberate, unnecessary actions of thoughts that stimulate sexually outside of a marriage situation are wrong.

Firstly, it is very important to have a right understanding of sex. In this country, our attitudes vary from the prudish, depressing view that all sexual drives and instincts are degrading signs of weakness and that marriage is a toleration of this weakness and a necessary evil. This view is a sad reflection on the education and upbringing that produced it. It mars many an otherwise potentially happy marriage.

The other extreme that, unfortunately, is becoming all too prevalent among modern "enlightened" people is that of the person who sees sex as a personal possession whose use is nobody else's business except his own, and who believes that he or she is entitled to sexual pleasure whenever they feel like it, irrespective of any consequences.

The truth is that the procreative power is the most God-like power man possesses. God creates, and the nearest man comes to that is by procreation. It is a tremendous power. God didn't have to give it to us. He could have arranged things differently, but He chose to share His creative power with mankind and thus gave us the beautiful institutions of marriage and parenthood.

Sex, by its nature, is something good, sacred and holy. It is not tawdry or sordid. It is something to be proud of and something to possess and guard jealously. When we use our sexuality in accordance with God's will, we honour Him and glorify Him. When we misuse and abuse it and cheapen it, we offend Him.

In order to ensure continuance of the human race, God implanted certain instincts and drives in each of us and favoured their fulfilment with certain pleasurable feelings. It is important to be aware of our own sexuality and not to deny or ignore it or be afraid of it. It is important, particularly for young people , that they be prepared for their sexual awakening and that they recognise and accept the usual changes and feeling in their bodies as a normal part of their development.

All too often, I find young people, and boys particularly, going through a real trauma of conscience that would not be necessary if they had been given even a little forewarning and instruction on the process of becoming an adult.

For a young girl, the natural development is that she begins to produce eggs in her ovaries, and this gives rise to a physical process which will necessitate her mother or somebody else explaining it to her.

For boys, things are more difficult because things begin to happen which they don't fully understand, and they may develop habits which they enjoy while at the same time feeling they are wrong. They grope for knowledge and very often get it in the wrong quarters, because they are afraid to talk to a priest or parents who fool themselves by saying: "He hasn't asked me anything yet."

Things can be made even worse for a youngster when they

read only the objective laws which I stated in the beginning, or have it laid down to them coldly and bluntly, without any explanation or guidance. It is vitally important that young people should be given a correct view of sex and be prepared for their development which they should see as a natural part of the development of all normal people, including the Parish Priest and the Reverend Mother. It is important to give them a pride in the power God has given them, and the will to cherish it and to respond to God's trust by using it only in accordance with His Will.

For some people, sexual control is easy; for others, it is difficult. God knows and understand the sexuality with which He has endowed each one of us. He expects only our best efforts and allows for the situations we find ourselves in and our strength in temptation. Our best efforts should include an honest assessment of our own strength and a wholesome mistrust of taxing that strength too much. It is much easier and wiser to avoid the situation that gives rise to the temptation than it is to resist the temptation itself.

A good confessor in whom you have confidence can be a great help, particularly for people who get depressed and despair of their ability to cope with their sexuality.

Looking at the Seventh and Tenth Commandments

Just as I put the Sixth and Ninth Commandments together, so I will combine the Seventh and Tenth: "Thou shalt not steal" and "Thou shalt not covet thy neighbour's goods."

The Tenth Commandment forbids us to do in our thoughts what the Seventh forbids us to do in our actions. The only difference between dishonest thoughts and dishonest actions is that there is no "paying back" to do when dishonesty is confined to thought.

The Seventh Commandment demands that we practise the virtue of justice—that we give everyone his due.

The first and most obvious way we offend against justice is by stealing. Theft is the voluntary taking or keeping of something that belongs to another, against the owner's reasonable will.

The latter clause is an important one because it distinguishes borrowing from stealing and allows for other rare times when a greater need such as life itself overrules the right of an owner to his property.

I don't have to dwell on the sinfulness of stealing. It is universally understood and accepted.

However, there are many other ways of offending against justice. Unfortunately many of them are not seen to be sinful by people who blind themselves or excuse themselves by calling their actions "good business" or "accepted business practice".

The law of the land does not always guarantee moral justice:

while our prisons are full of petty thieves, there are many greater criminals walking around untouched and even protected by the civil law.

To deprive another by deceit or fraud of what is his, is cheating. To that category belong such practices as short weight, short measure, and misrepresenting merchandise, such as turning the clock back on a used car.

The whole business of buying and selling in this country is riddled with gimmicks and practices that are fraudulent and sinful. It's amazing that "good practising Catholics" sin daily in this way without batting an eyelid.

The abuse and misuse of government schemes and grants by falsifying specifications or switching cattle cards, or working without stamping insurance cards and drawing the dole, is not only practised on a grand scale but is also admired and lauded in many instances.

It is a form of cheating, too, for an employer to underpay his workers, particularly when scarcity of work enables him to do this. It is equally wrong for a worker to deliberately "doss" or waste materials or present a certificate for a fake illness.

Even more sophisticated, less detectable types of fraud can be committed by solicitors and government officials, bankers and others in specialised positions of power, where the lack of professional knowledge and expertise makes the ordinary citizen an easy victim.

The sort of deceit I'm thinking of is reflected in the case of the doctor who sent a patient to a specialist carrying a sealed envelope. The patient, out of curiosity, opened the envelope and the note it contained said simply: "I'm sending you a fat goose; pluck it well!"

Politicians and officials in state and semi-state bodies are in specially privileged positions to be dishonest if they wish, and again it can be all so legal that they nearly fool themselves too that they are honest people.

Bribes and back-handers for grants, planning permission,

etc. are seen as perks of the job by people who would never dream of putting their hands directly into somebody's pocket.

Bankers and receivers have such unquestionable powers that they have a special obligation to be careful never to abuse or misuse them.

There are two other ways in which we can offend against justice, namely receiving stolen property and keeping found property without making reasonable efforts to restore it to its rightful owner.

My only comment is that I believe receivers are more contemptible than the thieves, and indeed without receivers we would have very few thieves.

True sorrow for sins against the Seventh Commandment can only be genuine when it includes a sincere intention to make restitution as fully and quickly as possible. A person may not profit from his own dishonesty. Even when it is not possible to make restitution to the hurt party or his heirs, then the illicit gains must be given to some genuine charitable cause.

We cannot measure moral evil by a yardstick or compute it on an adding machine, so it is not possible to give absolute figures or amounts that constitute mortal sin.

A number of relative factors must be taken into account. However, most rational people are quite well able to decide in their own conscience when they have sinned gravely and if they sincerely require guidance in the matter of restitution they can always consult their confessor.

In conclusion, I would remind readers that we are all answerable for our own actions. It is no excuse to be dishonest in any way simply because it is an accepted practice in the trade or profession or because "everybody else is doing it".

Bearing False Witness

Every one of us should think seriously about the Eighth Commandment: "Thou shalt not bear false witness against thy neighbour."

This commandment, apart from forbidding calumny, forbids a number of other allied offences. The main ones are detraction, personal insult, tale-bearing and lying.

Calumny is the worst offence against this commandment because it combines sins against truthfulness, justice and charity. To tell a lie about someone is to hurt him where the pain is keenest—in his reputation. If I steal his money he will be angry, but he can earn more or I can restore it when I repent. When I cast a shadow on a man's good name, I have robbed him of something precious that all the sweat in the world may not be able to restore, and that I may never be able to replace, no matter how repentant I am. Words once spoken can never be fully recalled. The damage is aggravated by the unfortunate willingness of people to believe the bad story and to retell it, and undoubtedly exaggerate it in the retelling. Needless to say, calumny under oath becomes perjury.

Even if I know something discreditable about my neighbour that is in fact true, I commit the sin of detraction by retelling it unnecessarily, if it is not common knowledge already. There are, of course, times when we have a duty to reveal someone's faults to certain people, such as a parent or teacher or boss or the police, for the purpose of prevention or correction, but we must be sure that our motives are the correct ones. Very often we begin by saying: "I think I ought to tell you this . . ." when in fact it would be more honest to say: "I'm dying to tell you this."

We can offend against this commandment with our ears, too. It is wrong to listen willingly to slander or detraction, even though we may say nothing ourselves. Our very silence is an encouragement to the malicious gossiper.

Personal insult is another common offence. In speech or in action, we offend our neighbour when we refuse him the marks of decent respect or friendship that are due to him, such as ignoring an outstretched hand or speaking to him rudely or abusively.

Tale-bearing is one of the common curses of this country. It does untold damage to marriages, family bonds, business and all kinds of other important relationships. There are many people who consider themselves good Catholics and who are faithful to all their religious duties and who would never dream of stealing, killing or committing adultery yet, when it comes to gossip and tale-bearing, they are champions. They usually start by "I think you ought to know . . ." In fact, it would be much better if Mick never knew what crack Jack made about him, particularly when it is taken out of context. The tale-bearers of Ireland may get a rude shock when they face St. Peter. They may have to take their place in the queue behind a lot of others with whom they "wouldn't be seen dead" in this life.

Finally we come to lying. Lying is never good. Anytime we use God's gift of speech to tell a lie, we abuse it and offend Him. Obviously the gravity of the offence will depend on the gravity of the matter we lie about, how many times, and the gravity of the effect of that lie.

The one occasion when we can lawfully tell a falsehood is when someone is unjustly trying to get the truth from us. It is a lawful means of self defence when there is no other alternative. We are not obliged always either to tell all the truth. Some nosey people ask questions which they have no right to ask and we are entitled to give them evasive answers. There are also some conventional phrases which might appear to be lies but are not, because all intelligent people understand what they really mean.

A final possible sin against the Eighth Commandment is the revealing of a secret which has been entrusted to me. The obligation to secrecy may arise from a promise made or my profession as a doctor, lawyer, etc. There would have to be good and grave reasons for breaking such secrecy.

Whatever our sin is against the Eighth Commandment, we are always bound to restitution. For true repentance I must always intend, and try, to the best of my ability to repair the damage done by me. The sad thing is that it is rarely possible, even with the best efforts, to undo the hurt caused by slander or detraction.

The Eighth Commandment is the one most frequently broken. A good rule for all of us is to keep our mouths shut unless we are saying what we honestly believe to be true and never to speak even the truth about our neighbour unless it is to his credit or is called for because of some grave reason.

Living in the Shadow of the Gunmen

Patriotism is a fine and noble thing when it means love of one's country—but it is a sickness when it means hating others, and a madness when it causes people to turn violently on their own.

I am as Irish as any man among us. As a boy, I was thrilled by the stories of the Fianna and Cuchulainn, Patrick Sarsfield and Red Hugh O'Donnell.

But it was their bravery and chivalry that thrilled me—and these are qualities that are singularly lacking in our so-called patriots today.

What bravery and chivalry is involved in the countless murders and bank raids, knee cappings and bombing that the IRA so proudly claim responsibility for today?

I know I can be given a long list of atrocities perpetrated by the "other side". But two wrongs don't make a right. No matter what atrocities are committed, it is no excuse to descend to the same level of animal behaviour.

The UFF, the IRA and all other paramilitary organisations, make me totally sick with their play-acting at being soldiers, when, in fact, they are nothing more than gangsters and thugs—and cowardly ones at that.

When Jessie James robbed a bank, he admitted he was a thief and claimed no noble motives. He also had to face men equipped with guns.

When our terrorists shoot and bomb innocent civilians, they face no danger, yet expect us all to salute them as our patriotic saviours.

The people who really make me sick, however, are the people who shelter behind the political wings of these groups, both Protestant and Catholic.

These are the people who, in safety, incite others to play the patriot game and provoke them to do the dirty work. They are the people who should bear the real guilt for the deeds of the young people whose minds they poison and warp.

These are the people who preach freedom and at the same time deny it to all who disagree with them. There are many good Catholics in the North who will tell you in whispers that, while they can get on well with their Protestant neighbours, their real fear is of their bully-boy self-appointed Provo protectors.

I cross the Border regularly and it angers me somewhat to be held up by foreign soldiers in my own country.

I don't even like to see the red pillar boxes that symbolise British rule there.

I'd love to see a united Ireland, but not at the cost of one innocent life. No piece of land is worth the shedding of innocent blood. I'd rather see Ulster peaceful and prosperous under British rule than bloodied and torn with hatred as it is now.

When will our blind patriots learn that you can't force people at the point of a gun to love you? You can only hope some day to win their love with your own love, patience, tolerance and sacrifice.

Probably the sickest people of all are the "public house patriots" here in the Republic. They go to Mass on Sunday and then, from the safety of a quiet country pub, expostulate to gullible young listeners about the "Boys" and what they should do in England and the North.

Some even stick their chests out heroically as they sell their subversive papers and shake their collection boxes for "the cause".

Apart from the cowardice, the hurt to the innocent and the sheer stupidity and debasing brutality of most of our "heroes" activities, it is my duty to point out that it is a grave mortal sin to engage in or support any of those terrorist acts.

No matter how much you blind yourself, murders by the I.R.A. are your sins also, if you contribute one penny through collections or the purchase of subversive publications.

Your pennies purchase the bullets and the machine guns that are so often turned even on our own unarmed police.

It's time we all got our priorities right, and stood up to be counted. It's time we recalled the words of Christ himself: "What does it profit a man to gain the whole world (let alone Ulster) and suffer the loss of his own soul?"

Handing On the Faith

I recently found myself at two meetings which discussed much the same topic, namely, handing on the faith to our young people.

There was much criticism of modern teaching methods and of the influence of television and the media. There was obvious concern about the direction young people were taking, whether they were chasing pleasure through the abuse of drink, drugs and sex, or seeking answers in new philosophies or sects. I have been at many similar discussions in recent times. While I don't dispute the validity or sincerity of many of the points of concern and criticism made, I do feel that we avoid the main issue, which is to examine our own consciences individually as adults and to ask ourselves whether we have a faith ourselves to hand on and, if so, whether it is visible and attractive in our daily lives.

There is no doubt that there is need for better teaching methods and programmes. Many false principles and ideals are being propagated glamorously and glibly through the media, but the most important element in passing on the faith is that we practise what we preach sincerely. The end product should be a life-style and performance that appeals to young people.

Young people in general are idealistic. They reject hypocrisy and sham and are attracted by sincerity, honesty and enthusiasm. It is a sobering thought that the rapid growth of the early church was attributed not so much to the inspired preaching of the apostles as the attractive life-style of the early Christians. They lived their faith, and the sincere application of Christian principles in their lives caused pagan observers to exclaim: "See how those Christians love one another." This roused in them a desire to investigate and share in this happy living.

There are many young people today who don't know God because their parents are part of a *nouveau riche* who think they can fly without God. Money and material things are their gods. They are the sort of people who would fit well into the Dallas scene. Their faith is dead or dormant and when their children get involved in drugs or drink they wonder why.

There are many other young people whose parents consider themselves to be God-fearing and practising Christians and also wonder why their children seek fulfilment in other directions. Outside influences may contribute to this, but such parents must have an honest look at the image they present in their own lives to their children.

It is one thing to practise routine Christian exercises, but it is another thing to live Christianity. Christ gave us Mass, prayer and the sacraments as aids to Christian living and, unless our Mass-going and praying and other spiritual exercises produce a real Christian performance in our own lives, we cannot expect young people to believe that they will be of any value to them.

What we must ask ourselves is: do we really know what we are doing ourselves or are we simply going through traditional and comforting exercises? If your child asked you why you go to Mass, could you give him a sincere and worthwhile answer? Does he see you accepting God's will when it demands sacrifice or hurts you?

Is your religion a comfortable coat that you inherit and wear as long as it is comfortable and doesn't pinch? Is it something that is a part of you yourself, and that you couldn't discard or ignore no matter how much it pinches?

The Church itself has much to answer for. We have done a lot with out liturgy but we have fallen down badly on preaching the word of God. If our vocations are down, then priests, nuns and religious must ask themselves why young people are no longer attracted to serve God in this way. Do they no longer seem relevant?

The state too seems to be hell-bent on divorcing its business from Christian living. Economics, political expediency, vote-catching, etc. are all still very real factors in determining government policy and action. When Christian principles are mentioned, we are told that these are a matter for individual consciences.

Trade unions, farmers, publicans, teachers, gardai and many other responsible bodies must look at the example they are giving to young people. Civil disobedience and threats to authority are regular practices nowadays in the mad scramble to achieve our own rights, and it is a very rare thing nowadays for a young person to hear of any person or organisation talking of their Christian *obligations* rather than their *rights*.

We may worry about handing on the faith and about outside influences, but we must first worry about our own faith and how visibly and attractively it shines through our own daily living. If young people like the cake we offer them, then they will be interested in the recipe.

Finding Answers
in the Rosary

I would dearly love to see the Rosary restored to its rightful place in Irish life. Any form of prayer that gets you through to God is good but the Rosary is something special. The fact that the Church gives it, and no other form of prayer, a feast of its own—the Feast of the Holy Rosary—is an indication of the value placed on it and earned by it over centuries.

When no army could save Europe, the Rosary did. When neither priest or Mass was available, the Rosary kept the faith and courage of the Irish people alive. Indeed, the Rosary should have a very special place in our national affections.

There are many who scoff at it as old-fashioned or ritualistic. Those who do so, don't know what it is all about.

The Rosary is the prayer of Mary. It does what she always did. It points us towards her Son, increases our love for Him by focusing our attention on His loving deeds for us, and urges us to be loyal followers of Him.

The clicking of beads and the repetition of Hail Mary's would be boring if there was nothing else to it, but these are only a way of measuring out a length of time spent meditating on events that should stir us, shame us, urge us and motivate us in our love of God and our service of Him through our fellow men. The strength of the prayer is in its simplicity. Anyone can use it. For the time taken to say ten "Hail Mary's", one is asked to meditate on one of fifteen important events in the lives of Christ and his Mother.

The Annunciation reminds us of the fulfilment of God's promise and gives us the example of Mary's acceptance of

God's will. The Visitation shows Mary's concern for someone other than herself and her willingness to put her own problems aside in order to help her cousin. The selfish among us could well benefit from some time spent thinking about it.

The Finding in the Temple has a big lesson for young people who think their parents are old-fashioned.

The Agony in the Garden gives courage to those who may find the will of God difficult to accept.

The Crucifixion can give courage to victims of violence and hatred.

The Resurrection gives new meaning to life and death.

The Assumption and Coronation of Our Lady show the reward for fidelity and trust in God in even the darkest hours of life.

I suggest that, for a start, families particularly could share some thoughts together each day on just one mystery and then meditate on those thoughts while reciting one decade.

Mary is a Special Saint

Not so long ago I received a pretty nasty crank letter. Of course it was anonymous. It was, in general, an attack on the Catholic Church, accusing us of worshipping idols. In particular it attacked our idolisation of Mary, the mother of Jesus Christ. I don't usually bother about anonymous letters but this one did raise some points that it might do no harm to clear up.

We believe that there is only one God. We worship Him and Him alone. We believe that we are all called to share an eternity of happiness with Him but the choice is ours. Either we love God and try to live our lives according to His will, or we reject God's will and pursue our own merry way in life.

Those who die in God's love go to heaven and are known to us as saints. Every soul that goes to heaven is a saint, but the Church from time to time publicly proclaims the certainty that some outstanding individual is a saint. This can lead us to believe that saints are a special elite group. In fact, the saints that the church proclaims and honours are just special saints.

Such saints were people who got special graces from God. The Church thanks God for the work they did and puts them before us as an example of how we all should try to cooperate with God's grace. They are also ambassadors in heaven. As our ambassadors and intercessors in heaven we pray through them to God. We can pray directly to God, but some people in their humility prefer, as in this life, to go through somebody else. Our prayers, when directed to a saint, are prayers for intercession.

Colloquially we talk of praying to St. Joseph or St. Maria Goretti and we talk of St. Jude getting us our requests. This can seem to indicate that we have set up some saint as another

God, but that is not so. Our prayers go to God through the saints and the graces we receive come from God through their intercession.

We believe that God grants special favours from time to time through a particular saint, as a sign of His approval and special love for that saint.

Mary is a special saint among special saints. As the mother of God she was the most perfect of the human race. She was preserved free from original sin, and we are proud of her and are inspired by her. She is our most influential intercessor. As our mother, she is our most compassionate and caring intercessor. She is also our best model and example of faith in God's love for us.

What makes Mary particularly special to us, apart from the fact that she is in a most powerful position as mother of God, is that one can easily identify with her and aim to follow her. She worked no miracles, wrote no books, founded no religious orders. She simply did what we are all called to do. She accepted God's will and carried it out to the best of her ability with an unwavering faith in its purpose.

Her faith was tested from the beginning. She believed that she was to be the mother of our Saviour. It was astounding and incredible but wonderful news. It must have been hard to believe, but it got even harder as things worked out. She surely could expect some place better than a stable as His birth-place and a joyful proclamation of His arrival rather than a hasty flight to Egypt.

When Christ grew through his twenties she must have wondered when he would move towards his kingship; when he did move towards the lakes of Galilee and people like Mary Magdalene, she must have been puzzled.

When Christ returned to Nazareth and was ejected from the temple, and when finally he was scourged and crucified, she had every reason to believe that a cruel joke had been played on her. Yet she remained tranquil and steadfast in her faith.

It was Mary who kept the apostles together when their faith was wavering and almost shattered. Is it any wonder that we call her the mother of the Church? God used her as the vehicle through which our Saviour came on earth, as the vehicle through which His church was born and over the years the vehicle through which much help has been given to the church in times of crisis. Her prayer of the rosary saved Europe and it kept the faith alive in this country too.

We don't worship anyone but God, but we make no apology for commemorating, celebrating and praying through our saints. In particular, we are proud of our sister Mary who became our mother and the mother of our Saviour. May our prayer always be: "Holy Mary, Mother of God, pray for us sinners."

Our Father: The Prayer Christ Gave Us

Basically, prayer is communication with a friend. I don't recommend any particular form of prayer, because the important thing is to get through to God in whatever way you care. Some formal prayers, however, can be helpful and none better than the one given to us by Christ himself.

If you could say one "Our Father" slowly and thoughtfully every day, it would have a very definite effect on your life and your relationship with God.

Our Father who art in heaven

This phrase immediately reminds us of Who we are praying to and where He is. It lifts our eyes and hearts to heaven, away from perishable earthly concerns to the beauty and eternity of another superior and more desirable life. It reminds us of the goal and purpose of our earthly lives and prevents us from concentrating too much on our earthly goals. Above all, it reminds us that God is a father who cares for us, protects us, guides us and loves us with an infinite wisdom, patience and love.

It helps us to accept the ups and downs of life with the calmness and tranquillity of a trusting child in its father's arms. I place my hand in God's hand and go wherever He leads me because I know that He loves me and could not lead me anywhere that wasn't ultimately in my best interests.

Hallowed be Thy name

My first duty is to praise God for His goodness and to show my gratitude, respect, reverence and love. I do this by honouring and praising His name, and by my desire that it should always be used with respect and reverence. Do I always live up to this obligation? Do I always use the name of God reverently and lovingly? Do I at times actually blaspheme and dishonour it?

Thy kingdom come
If I really love God I will want His dearest wishes to be fulfilled. I will want His kingdom of love and peace to grow among men. I will do joyfully what I can towards this end. Again, when I pray those words, I must ask myself if I am sincere, particularly when I think of the many times when I actually worked against this end by my selfishness and lack of love and actual deliberate hurt to others.

Thy will be done on earth, as it is in heaven
These are the words and wish of a person who genuinely knows God and loves Him. I must question my own sincerity when I pray them. How important is God's will and how hard do I try to implement it in my daily life? Can I too say like Jesus in Gethsemane: "Not my will, but Thine, O Lord"?

Give us this day our daily bread
This is perhaps the easiest part of our prayer, because we are all quite concerned about having our own needs supplied. We can all rattle off a list of requests, but I must ask myself if my motives are right and if indeed the things I ask for are for the benefit of my immortal soul or the souls for whom I pray. A little reflection on this phrase will help me to get my priorities right and to conquer my own selfishness.

And forgive us our trespasses
If I feel in any way proud or conceited, a little thought here should bring me down to earth again. If I feel that God has given me a raw deal, then I can't complain when I think of the

many times I have offended, neglected and let Him down. Indeed I must feel very humble and very much loved by God when I think of the infinite patience He has shown in repeatedly forgiving me and accepting promises that I have made and broken so often before.

As we forgive those who trespass against us
Christ must have had a sense of humour when He gave us this phrase! When I think of how easily I can feel hurt and how high and mighty I can become with those who hurt me and how slow I am to forgive them for the pettiest or even imaginary offences, it's a shock to realise that I am in fact asking God to give me the same grudging sort of forgiveness, or maybe even not to forgive me at all. Perhaps I should first give a little thought to those whom I should forgive before I ask God so blandly and expectantly to forgive me my much greater offences. I remember Christ's words: "If you have anything against your brother, leave your gift at the altar and go first and be reconciled with him."

And lead us not into temptation
God doesn't lead us into temptation and probably a better translation here would be "allow us not." I think of my poor resistance to temptation and I realise that very often my misdemeanours are due to deliberate and selfish desires rather than weakness in an undesired situation. I must question my own sincerity in praying those words and I must honestly assess my efforts to know my weaknesses and to curb them, and to avoid putting too much strain on them by keeping out of temptation. Reflection here must make me feel humble and much more tolerant of the failings of others.

Deliver us from evil
I want to love God. I am weak and at times afraid of the evil things I may meet in my life. I ask God to keep a firm hold on

my hand and always to steer me clear of the many pitfalls that may cause me to stumble or even fall. I ask God to do the same for those I love and indeed for those I should love and perhaps don't love as I ought.

The key to prayer is that you see God as a father, friend and lover who knows you intimately and with whom there is no need or point in "putting on an act". Be yourself. Relax with Him whenever, however and wherever you will. If you do feel a little out of touch then try an "Our Father" slowly and thoughtfully. It provides a framework for thoughts that must lead you nearer to God and give you a greater awareness of His presence.

Our Joy On
St. Patrick's Day

St. Patrick's Day is a feast day to which we all look forward. And not just in Ireland, either, for it is a day which is celebrated all over the world. In America everyone wants to be Irish for St. Paddy's Day and the same is true in Canada, Australia and New Zealand. It's a big get-together time also for our missionaries and Irish emigrants, whether they be in Hong Kong, Ethiopia or Alaska. It's a time when we Irish forget our self criticism and moaning and are proud to be Irish.

The feast of our national saint brings out the Irish nationalism and pride in us, but it should do something more. I can't help feeling that we have come to regard the day as being more important than the saint or that we regard him more as a patriot than as a man who brought Christ and his love to us.

Even the sight of the shamrock is more likely to evoke songs of Ireland than praise to God for the great miracle and mystery of the Trinity that it originally illustrated.

I wouldn't wish at all to play down the celebration of the occasion or the pride, memories and nostalgia, but I do think we should think a little harder about the man whose feast we are celebrating and about the reasons why we are grateful and originally honoured him as our patron.

It's amazing how little the average Irish person knows about St. Patrick and how little he figures in our prayers.

If there were pop charts kept of the saints he would figure way down on the Irish list behind Padre Pio, St. Jude and St. Martin de Porres. If we believe in the intercessory powers of the saint, then the saint who first brought the faith to Ireland

81

should be the one most concerned about interceding for us. Indeed, all our Irish saints from Columcille and Bridget to Oliver Plunkett and Matt Talbot have very little place in our prayers and very little of our confidence when we seek intercession. The only explanation I can think of is that it is a reflection of an Irish inferiority complex or a case of a prophet having no honour in his own country.

When we think of Patrick we should think with deep gratitude of the debt we owe to him for the sacrifices he made and the hardship he endured and the love he showed in bringing Christ to a people who had kidnapped him and treated him so harshly. Just as Christ brought life to a hostile world, so Patrick brought life to Ireland and it is that which we should be celebrating.

Far from singing rebel songs and remembering past hurts and old enmities, we should be on our knees thanking God for the precious gifts St. Patrick brought us and praying that we may receive the grace to follow Patrick's example of faith, love and forgiveness.

If St. Patrick's Day evokes pride, it should be a pride in our forefathers, who were wise enough to appreciate the gift of Patrick and strong enough to preserve it and hand it on through the roughest of times.

We should have pride, too, in the deeds and courage of our saints and missionaries, who brought this gift to so many other countries and generously shared it with so many other people. St. Patrick's Day should be a time for thanksgiving, appreciation and renewal and particularly it should be a time of forgiveness and healing.

If I appreciate fully the gift that God gave to my country in St. Patrick and if I appreciate fully the gift that St. Patrick brought to us, then I will thank both God and St. Patrick in the only really valid and sincere way, by putting these gifts to work in my own life.

So Much Good in the Worst of Us . . .

I do a radio programme each night Monday to Friday on 98FM. One of the features of the programme is the volume of mail I get from prisoners, as well as the use their relatives make of the programme to send greetings through me to the prisoners.

Recently a reaction has set in and a lot of people tell me I make too much of criminals. I am too soft on them, they tell me, and some refer to them as animals and thugs.

I am well aware of the effects of crime. On several occasions I have not only expressed sympathy to victims of crime but I have interviewed them and asked criminals to think of he deeper and more lasting traumatic effects of their crimes.

However, two wrongs don't make a right. It will not reduce the hurts they do or reduce crime itself to condemn all criminals as blackguards and evil people. Many of them are themselves victims of abuse, deprivation, and the more sophisticated crimes that society inflicts daily on the poor.

It is significant that the vast majority of our prison population comes from the poorer classes.

Recently I ran a poetry competition for the prisoners and even though I had often been moved by some of their letters I was still amazed at the quality of the entries and the feelings they expressed about subjects as varied as drug addiction, remorse, abortion, loneliness, mothers, a bird in the window or an insect on the wall. The only anger apparent was at the tendency of the public to condemn them all out of hand.

There are those who will always be criminals, but many will never return to prison again if they get the right help and understanding. An interesting feature of the letters I get is that most of them are happy with the prison staff but are angry with the Department of Justice for failing to implement the recommendations of the Whitaker Report. In particular, I would have to say that the facilities for women in our prisons are very poor. Even the staff there are doing time in a gloomy, archaic institution.

There is a lot of talent in our prisons and there are a lot of good people there, but they have very few opportunities to make use of their time to prepare to take their place as useful citizens when they return to society.

Apart from the lack of facilities, the biggest obstacle to rehabilitation is the attention of the media who are too ready to highlight any mistakes or softness in the Christian treatment of prisoners.

The people in our jails are the ones who are caught. We weren't. The criminal on the cross responded to Christ's love and I have found that most of our prisoners will respond to love also. There is so much good in the worst of us and so much bad in the best of us, that none of us is entitled to condemn the rest of us.

One of the marvellous qualities of Christ was His presumption of good in even the apparently worst people. Mary Magdalene, the thief on the cross, and Matthew the tax-collector, were all people who were presumed by common opinion to be bad, but Christ saw and loved the goodness in them. He reached out to them through the reputations and presumptions and found unerringly the soft responsive spot.

It is important that we Christians must, while condemning crime, continue to view criminals through the eyes of Christ and with the love of Christ, never seeing them as totally bad or lost and always trying to find and arouse that image of Christ in which undoubtedly every soul is made.

I've given more than one retreat in Mountjoy. I've been there several times, but it is always a very sobering and balancing experience as it gives me a view of the other side to the criminal. I can tell you Christ lives and is loved very deeply there. Many are forgotten and despised and some know that the only friend left is Jesus.

Here are the unedited words written by a man with a long prison record. Read them and then try to tell me he is all bad and lost.

Jesus help me to change my life
Jesus help me to see the light
Jesus start right here tonight
Jesus help me to understand the people in charge of me
Jesus I know, I know, I love thee
Jesus help me to make peace with my foe
Jesus help me more and more
Jesus I hurt you so bad
Jesus now I feel so mad
Jesus give me faith and strength
Jesus help me to repent
Jesus I love you I really do
Jesus I need you I really do
Jesus touch me once with your mighty hand
Jesus then I will understand
Jesus you know how sorry I am
Jesus my Lord take my hand
Jesus let the people be happy within these walls
Jesus let them know you own them all
Jesus you died for me on Calvary
Jesus my Lord never part from me
Jesus watch over me every day
Jesus my Lord I now pray
Jesus we know that you will forgive us
Jesus we know because you are with us
Jesus be with me night and day
Jesus I love you won't you stay

Jesus be always in my heart
Jesus my Lord never depart
Jesus my Lord I plead with Thee
Jesus be near and always with me
Jesus make me happy once more
Jesus you know I adore you so
Jesus I love you for ever more.

The Vineyard Waits

"The harvest is great but the labourers are few."

These words were never more true than they are today. Millions of people are sick, tired, and bewildered by the unrest, injustices, strikes, protests, discrimination, bullying and all the other unlovely things that they see every day in a very selfish and discontented world.

Some see no hope because they have not even the basic means of survival. Others have more than their share of material goods but are equally hopeless, because they find no satisfaction or real happiness in their material wealth.

The world needs God and His love and His soothing and hopeful words and guidance and promises, very badly, but the sad thing is that the agents of His gifts are all too few. There is a grave and urgent need for a big increase in vocations to the priesthood and religious life.

Every bishop is crying out for more priests. Many convents are closing down or amalgamating, rather than spreading their activities, through lack of nuns. Brothers and monasteries have the same problem. Yes indeed, there is a great and ripe harvest, but the labourers are all too few and becoming fewer.

All of us should pray that God will send more labourers into His vineyard. It is a good thing that people are becoming more conscious of their own lay priesthood. There has been a welcome increase in the involvement of lay people in the ministry of the Church, but there will always be a need for that special ministry that can only be exercised by those who have received

87

the Sacrament of Holy Orders and for religious who give their lives totally to the service of God.

Whether I be a priest, nun or lay person, I must be concerned about vocations if I have a proper love for God and a desire to share that love with others.

Our first duty is to pray for vocations. Christ himself asked us to do that. Over and above that I must ask myself what positive things I can do to foster vocations or help to bring them to fruition. Thank God, the day of pressurised or "mother's vocation" is gone, but if anything the unwanted pressures are there still but working in reverse now.

I was never pressurised. The priesthood was always presented to me as one of the ways of life open to me that was good and honourable and useful. I got a jolt recently when I asked an altar-boy if he would like to be a priest. His reply was: "You must be mad. Sure I'd have all the oul wans giving out about me then."

In Ireland particularly, where the priest was such a necessary and reassuring figure in community life, a new so-called, enlightened, pseudo-intellectual society is no longer so dependent on him. Indeed it has become fashionable to try to be totally independent of the priest.

The people who, when it suited, put the priest on a dizzy pedestal, are now busy knocking him off it. Children growing up in that atmosphere and exposed through sensation-seeking media to all our anti-clerics and anti-Christs can hardly find themselves attracted to religious life or see it as being very relevant.

The atmosphere in which the seed of a vocation is most likely to grow is that which obtains in a good and happy family where prayer and religious practice are a regular and normal part of life, and actually show results in love, happiness and service. Forced prayers, piety, and hypocrisy will hinder rather than help. Catholic magazines and papers available in a home will allow young people to become acquainted with and possibly admire the work of the church and the relevance of religious vocations.

I only wish some young people could meet the priests and nuns on the missions and see their work. They would certainly appreciate their relevance and recognise the need and the challenge.

This is no time for false humility. Priests and nuns should talk proudly of their work, not for their own sake, but to counteract the criticism and many misinformed and misleading brick-bats that are regularly thrown at them.

What I'm saying to my fellow clergy is: "Go public." Don't hide your light under a bushel. Be a light to the young. Let them know you and your concern and your work. Only then are they likely to admire and to follow.

Some recent developments give a little hope. Vocation seminars have been run at several venues and the attendances have been very good. At these seminars groups of young people can hear talks and hold discussions on the whole notion of the Christian vocation as well as the religious vocation.

They meet lay people, doctors, psychologists, and others, as well as representatives of the various religious orders so that they can examine fully the implications, responsibilities and variations of a vocation without any fear of pressure and indeed with a lot of good fun. Another good development is that many communities and orders welcome young people to come during their holidays to experience and live the life of the community, without any pressure to make a commitment.

The results of such seminars and visits and consultations with vocations directors for most young people is that they are reassured that in fact they have not a vocation and are not turning their backs on God's voice.

For boys who are interested in pursuing, or finally discarding, the stirrings of a vocation, there are vocations directors in every order or diocese, who will be very helpful.

Age and money are not problems. The important elements in a vocation are Attraction, Suitability, the Acceptance or Call, and the Free Response. Pray that the Lord will send more labourers and do what you can by word and example to help him do so.

Real Love Means Giving Not Taking

The message of Christ is still the only recipe for real happiness. Christ preached love but the love he preached and practised was unselfish giving and forgiving love. The love practised in the world today is self-love and it is paralysing society. At best it brings only temporary, fleeting satisfaction which, in its wake, leaves further longings, discontent, and other rainbows to be chased.

Christ was sent to do a job. He didn't just do that job. He didn't just earn for us a second chance of eternal happiness. He gave us all kinds of helps to insure that we would benefit from that chance. He gave us the wisdom of his teaching. He gave us the example of his own life. He gave us Mass and the sacraments. He taught us to pray. He gave us a Church to teach and guide us, that he promised would never fail, and would always enjoy the infallible guidance of the Holy Spirit.

Finally, he gave his life for us and, even as he hung there naked and dying, he was not thinking of his pain and suffering, but was still searching for other ways to love us. He forgave his executioners and, seeing his mother there, he gave her to us also.

Truly one could say: "Greater love than this, man cannot have." The hallmark of his love was the unselfish giving element and the lack of concern for the cost of it or for any reciprocation or gratitude.

For those of us who profess to be Christian, that is the model we must try to simulate. It will always involve a battle with our own human nature and it may seem too difficult even to attempt, but the rewards are great, not only in the next life but here and now. The happy people I know are the unselfish people who care and give so much to their families, friends, and others that they haven't time to think of themselves.

I meet them daily in my work. They have a peace and serenity that money couldn't buy. They can be rich, poor or middle class. What does the trick for them is their attitude to life and their awareness of God and His love. They accept God's will and see themselves as being put here to serve rather than be served. They thank God for what He has given them and never complain about the things He hasn't given them. Could any wealth, power or position give what people like Mother Teresa have got?

Selfishness is a cancer that is growing rapidly and destroying happiness. When power and wealth and material things take over from our spiritual goals, we lose our sense of direction and head for hell. I saw more happiness and contentment among the starving people in Uganda than I do on my visits to the well-fed wealthy capitals of the world. While the hungry laugh and sing and share a bowl of meal, we moan over the TV programmes and really get depressed if the video breaks down.

I see great lack of love in the paltry token-gestures made by our wealthy nations towards the third world. I have listened to businessmen moaning about the recession and, in the same breath, discussing their new villa in Spain, rather than worrying about the workers and their families who depend on them for jobs.

We see groups who have jobs negotiating deals that involve more money for them at the cost of the jobs of others.

We have our mighty tax dodgers too, and a general grab-all mentality with little care for morality or people at all levels of society.

The vandalism and brutality that we read of every day are but a symptom of the sickness that is growing among us.

We have a multiplicity of groups agitating for their rights

and prepared to trample on the rights of others to achieve them. The word "obligation" has disappeared from our vocabulary and the word "right" has changed its meaning to "might".

We have women's rights, civil rights, all kinds of rights, but we haven't got happiness.

Rights are important but they don't bring joy when they are *won* in battle. To be what they should be, they must be *given* with love.

"He Was a Good Man."

One of the problems of a big parish is that it is not possible to get to know all your parishioners. You can only hope that they can know you and know you well enough to come to you when they have problems.

I received a funeral recently and I didn't know the deceased person. I asked a neighbour who he was and I got a very interesting answer.

He said: "Ah Father, he was a good man."

He didn't say that he was a rich man or a poor man, a fat man, a thin man, a serious man or a gas man. He didn't say that he was a good singer or footballer or mention any other of his talents. Instinctively he said the one thing that was worth saying at that time—"He was a good man."

A funeral is an occasion when we get our priorities right. Attendance at a funeral, apart from the support it gives to the mourners, is a time for some sobering thoughts for ourselves. In many parishes it is the custom to provide confessions after the reception of the remains. It is a welcome facility for the immediate friends and relations to prepare for the funeral Mass, but quite often it is the occasion of a return to God of someone who has strayed for a long time from Him.

Life can be busy, hectic and exciting. There is so much to be done, achieved and enjoyed that we don't have time for God. We can have such material success that we don't feel the need for God. When a friend or relative dies, things change. Doctors, money, and no power on earth can do anything for him. We have to look elsewhere and the only place to look is to God.

We are consoled by our belief in an after-life and by Christ's promise that He has prepared a place for each of us. Our helplessness is relieved by the fact that we can pray for God's help and mercy. In our praying we grope for reasons why God should show His love and mercy. We discard the recommendations and qualities that we might use in a reference for a job or membership of a club but don't count now.

We come down to the simple recommendation: "He was a good man."

Sometimes we reduce that to : "He wasn't a bad man."

We come back to Christ's words on the cross: "Father, forgive them, for they know not what they do."

We may use other words like: "He meant no harm."

Funerals remind me of the inevitability of death. They remind me that we live only to die. No other event in our lives is more important. They prompt me to review my life and the things to which I devote my energies.

I ask myself how well prepared I am and what my friends could say if it were my own funeral. I'd be quite happy if they could say: "Lord, he was a good man."

I think of the many times I sinned or neglected or failed God—of the many times I was not prepared for death, but I take consolation from those words of Christ which indicate His love even for the sinner and the foolish excuses He is prepared to make for me. I have been lured often from God by a slick smart-aleck know-it-all world, but I thank God that I will be judged by Him and not by the same world which can be so pompous, self-righteous and unforgiving.

Next time you attend a funeral, remember that your own will come some day.

Will your friends be able to say confidently: "He was a good man"?